JUAN SOTO

BASEBALL SUPERSTAR

BY ANTHONY K. HEWSON

Copyright © 2025 by Press Room Editions. All rights reserved. No part of this book may be used or reproduced in any manner whatsoever, including internet usage, without written permission from the copyright owner, except in the case of brief quotations embodied in critical articles and reviews.

Book design by Jake Nordby
Cover design by Jake Nordby

Photographs ©: Brandon Sloter/Icon Sportswire/AP Images, cover, 1; Tim Warner/Getty Images Sport/Getty Images, 4; Elsa/Getty Images Sport/Getty Images, 7; Cliff Welch/Icon Sportswire, 8; Mike Janes/Four Seam Images/AP Images, 10; Greg Fiume/Getty Images Sport/Getty Images, 13; G. Fiume/Getty Images Sport/Getty Images, 14; Will Newton/Getty Images Sport/Getty Images, 16; Bob Levey/Getty Images Sport/Getty Images, 18; Sean M. Haffey/Getty Images Sport/Getty Images, 20–21; Patrick Smith/Getty Images Sport/Getty Images, 22; Denis Poroy/Getty Images Sport/Getty Images, 25; Gregory Fisher/Icon Sportswire/AP Images, 27, 30; Red Line Editorial, 29

Press Box Books, an imprint of Press Room Editions, Inc.

ISBN
978-1-63494-953-8 (library bound)
978-1-63494-967-5 (paperback)
978-1-63494-994-1 (epub)
978-1-63494-981-1 (hosted ebook)

Library of Congress Control Number: 2024940746

Distributed by North Star Editions, Inc.
2297 Waters Drive
Mendota Heights, MN 55120
www.northstareditions.com

Printed in the United States of America
012025

About the Author
Anthony K. Hewson is a freelance writer originally from San Diego. He and his wife now live in San Francisco with their two dogs.

TABLE OF CONTENTS

CHAPTER 1

Staying Alive 5

CHAPTER 2

Learning to Hit 9

CHAPTER 3

Postseason Hero 15

SPECIAL FEATURE

Going, Going, Gone 21

CHAPTER 4

Moving On 23

Timeline • 28
At a Glance • 30
Glossary • 31
To Learn More • 32
Index • 32

1 STAYING ALIVE

Juan Soto swung aggressively at a fastball. The Washington Nationals star fouled it straight back. Soto turned to Houston Astros catcher Robinson Chirinos. If that pitch had been a few inches lower, Soto said, he'd have hit it out of the park.

Game 6 of the 2019 World Series was tied 2–2. The Nationals trailed the series three games to two. They had to win this game to keep their season alive.

Juan Soto racked up nine hits during the 2019 World Series.

THE SOTO SHUFFLE

Juan Soto has an unusual routine between pitches. Sometimes he squats and moves from side to side. Then he swipes at the dirt with his leg. Soto's unique movements earned the nickname the "Soto Shuffle." Soto started doing it in the minor leagues. It helps him stay loose while hitting. He also thinks it distracts the pitcher.

Soto was only in his second season in the big leagues. Even so, pitchers already knew about his dangerous hitting skills. Soto watched another pitch. He didn't swing at this one. Houston ace Justin Verlander thought the pitch was a strike. Soto knew it wasn't. Ball, he told Chirinos.

Soto thought Verlander would try the same spot again. He was right. And this time, the pitch was a few inches lower. Soto didn't miss it. He hammered the ball deep. Verlander could only watch. The ball sailed into the right field stands for a home run.

Soto's home run in Game 6 was his third of the 2019 World Series.

Soto's blast gave the Nationals a 3–2 lead. They went on to win the game 7–2. Washington had forced a Game 7. Nats fans couldn't wait to watch their team play for its first World Series title. With Soto, anything seemed possible.

2 LEARNING TO HIT

Juan Soto was born on October 25, 1998. He grew up in the Dominican Republic. Juan started playing baseball at a young age. He didn't always practice with a baseball, though. Juan's dad would throw bottle caps for batting practice. And sometimes he used crumpled pieces of paper. That helped improve Juan's hand-eye coordination.

Juan didn't always have a bat, either. He and his brother, Elian, sometimes practiced with a broomstick. Not having a

Juan Soto started playing professional baseball in 2016.

bat and a baseball helped Juan. He had to use a thin broomstick to hit a tiny bottle cap. Hitting a baseball turned out to be much easier. When Juan started playing organized baseball, he rarely swung and missed.

By the time Juan was 16, Major League Baseball (MLB) teams already wanted to sign him. Experts ranked him as one of the top international prospects in baseball. The Washington Nationals signed him in 2015. The team gave Juan a $1.5 million contract.

Juan made his professional debut the next summer. As a 17-year-old, he started in the lowest level of the minor leagues. He was younger than most of his teammates. But Juan showed all the skills he'd learned as a youth

Juan Soto posted a batting average of .362 in the minor leagues.

player. He hit for a high average. He rarely struck out. And he got on base a lot.

Juan quickly advanced through the minor leagues. Injuries were the only thing that slowed him down. In 2017, he played only 32 games.

In 2018, Juan Soto moved to more competitive leagues twice. Then in May, one of Washington's outfielders suffered an injury. The Nationals called up Soto to replace him. At just 19 years old, he was the youngest player in MLB.

Soto made his MLB debut on May 20, 2018. He struck out in his only

THE YOUNGER SOTO

Juan Soto is seven years older than his brother, Elian. When Juan signed with the Nationals, Elian was only nine. Elian watched and learned from his older brother. Then Elian's turn came when he was 17. The Nationals signed him in January 2023. Elian made his minor league debut later that year.

Soto salutes Washington fans after his first MLB home run.

at-bat. The next day, he started for the first time. On the first pitch he saw, Soto smashed a home run.

After Soto returned to the dugout, the crowd kept cheering. He came back out to wave. Nationals fans couldn't get enough of their young superstar.

3 POSTSEASON HERO

Juan Soto put together a strong rookie season. He finished second in voting for National League (NL) Rookie of the Year. Nationals fans couldn't wait to see what he could do in his first full season.

Soto improved in 2019. He smashed 34 homers and drove in 110 runs that year. He helped the Nats win 11 more games than they did in 2018. That improvement helped them make the playoffs. Despite being just 20 years old, Soto played like a veteran. The Milwaukee Brewers were

Soto hit 22 home runs and drove in 70 runs as a rookie in 2018.

Washington's first opponent in the playoffs. The teams faced off in the NL Wild Card Game.

The Nationals trailed 3-1 in the bottom of the eighth inning. Time was running out on their season. With two outs and the bases loaded, Soto stepped to the plate. He had to face Milwaukee's star closer, Josh Hader. On a 1-1 count, Soto hit a laser to right field. All three runners scored. The Nationals advanced to the NL Division Series (NLDS) with a 4-3 win.

In the NLDS, Washington again faced a win-or-go-home situation. The Nationals trailed 3-1 late against the Los Angeles Dodgers. Soto's teammate Anthony Rendon hit a solo homer. Then Soto stepped to the plate against Dodgers ace Clayton Kershaw. On the first

Soto celebrates his game-winning hit in the 2019 NL Wild Card Game.

Soto does his signature "Soto Shuffle" during the 2019 World Series.

pitch, Soto hammered a home run to right center. That helped send Washington to the NL Championship Series (NLCS).

Soto had just three hits in the next round. But the Nationals still advanced to the World Series for the first time in team history. Soto had some big hits in the Fall Classic. None was bigger than his go-ahead homer in Game 6. That set the stage for the biggest game in team history.

The Nationals fell behind 2-0 in Game 7. Soto earned a walk in the seventh inning. Then his teammate hit a home run that gave the Nats a 3-2 lead.

In the eighth, Soto drove in a run with a hit. That gave his team some breathing room. Washington fans watched from back home as their team won its first championship. With Soto leading the way, they hoped there would be more to come.

DREAM COME TRUE

Game 3 of the 2019 World Series took place on October 25, 2019. That was Soto's 21st birthday. That day also confirmed a prediction that Soto's father had made. A decade earlier, Soto and his family were watching the World Series on his birthday. His father predicted that Soto would play in the World Series one day.

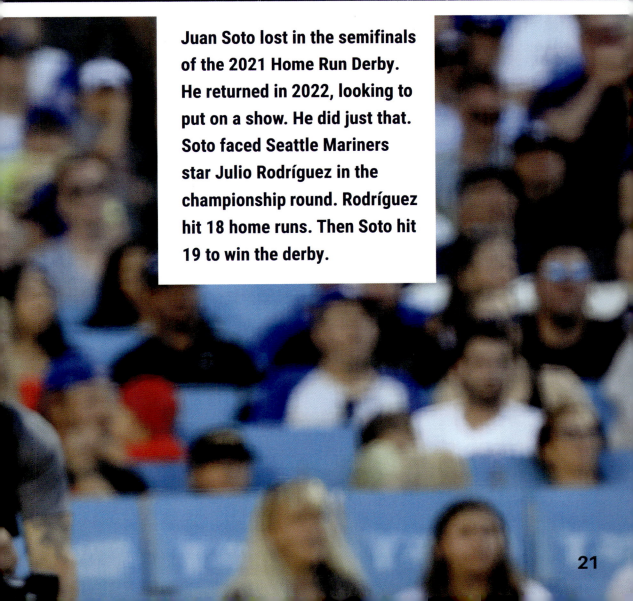

GOING, GOING, GONE

Juan Soto lost in the semifinals of the 2021 Home Run Derby. He returned in 2022, looking to put on a show. He did just that. Soto faced Seattle Mariners star Julio Rodríguez in the championship round. Rodríguez hit 18 home runs. Then Soto hit 19 to win the derby.

4 MOVING ON

Washington fans were ready for another championship run in 2020. But the COVID-19 pandemic pushed the start of the season back to July. The season lasted only 60 games. Soto made the most of the short season. He became the youngest batting champion in NL history. However, the Nationals missed the playoffs.

Few players had achieved what Soto had at his age. Boston Red Sox legend Ted Williams started his Hall of Fame

Soto hit for a career-high .351 batting average in 2020.

GIVING BACK

Soto appeared in his first All-Star Game in 2021. For making the game, Soto earned $200,000. Soto chose to donate that money to some of his fellow Dominican athletes. Soto helped fund the travel and training for athletes in that year's Summer Olympics. That included the country's baseball team, which won the bronze medal.

career at a young age. Williams's eye at the plate and hitting skills were similar to Soto's. Fans and experts began to think Soto might end up in the Hall of Fame one day.

Soto took another step in that direction in 2021. He finished second in NL Most Valuable Player (MVP) voting. After the season, Washington offered him a new contract. It would pay him $350 million over 13 years. Soto liked playing in Washington. But he wanted to wait until his current contract expired before signing a new one. He planned to see what other offers awaited him.

Soto recorded a hit and two walks in his debut with the Padres.

Rather than lose Soto for nothing, the Nationals chose to trade him during the 2022 season. He went to the San Diego Padres. They were in the middle of a playoff race. At first, Soto struggled on his new team. Then he came alive in the postseason.

The Padres trailed in Game 4 of the NL Division Series against the Dodgers. In the seventh inning, Soto stepped to the plate with the tying run on third. He laced the ball into right field, and the runner scored. The Padres went on to win the game and the series.

In 2023, Soto led the majors with 132 walks. He also smashed 35 homers. Both of those were among the best marks in Padres history. Soto's contract was set to expire after the 2024 season. The Padres made the same choice Washington did. Before the season, they traded Soto. This time, he went to the New York Yankees.

The move brought Soto to one of baseball's most famous teams. Soto joined an outfield that included superstar Aaron Judge. The Yankees hadn't won a title in 15 years. That's not a long

Soto hit seven home runs in his first month with the Yankees.

time for most teams. But for the Yankees, it felt like a century. The team now had one of the best players in the league. Fans hoped Soto could lead the team back to the World Series.

TIMELINE

1. Santo Domingo, Dominican Republic (October 25, 1998)
Juan Soto is born.

2. Boca Chica, Dominican Republic (July 2, 2015)
The Washington Nationals sign Juan to his first professional contract at the age of 16.

3. Viera, Florida (June 25, 2016)
Juan makes his pro baseball debut with the Gulf Coast Nationals.

4. Washington, DC (May 20, 2018)
Soto makes his MLB debut at 19 years old.

5. Houston, Texas (October 30, 2019)
Soto goes 2 for 4 in Game 7 of the World Series as the Nationals win their first championship.

6. Denver, Colorado (July 13, 2021)
Soto plays in his first MLB All-Star Game.

7. San Diego, California (August 3, 2022)
Soto plays his first game with the San Diego Padres.

8. Bronx, New York (April 5, 2024)
Soto plays his first home game as a member of the New York Yankees.

MAP

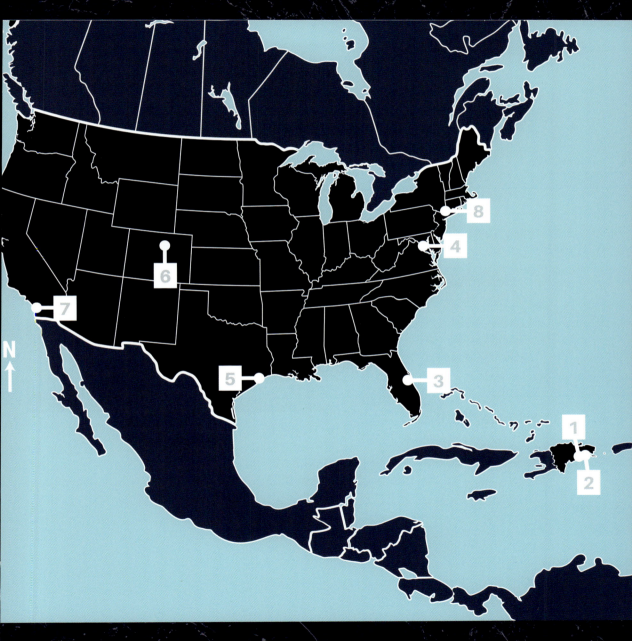

29

AT A GLANCE

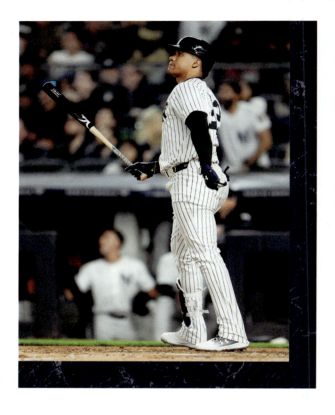

Birth date: October 25, 1998

Birthplace: Santo Domingo, Dominican Republic

Position: Outfielder

Throws: Left

Bats: Left

Size: 6-foot-2 (188 cm), 224 pounds (102 kg)

Current team: New York Yankees (2024–)

Previous teams: Washington Nationals (2018–22), San Diego Padres (2022–23)

Major awards: NL Batting Champion (2020), Silver Slugger (2020–23), All-Star (2021–24)

Accurate through August 2024.

GLOSSARY

ace
The best starting pitcher on a team.

batting champion
The player with the highest batting average in either the American League or National League in a season.

closer
A relief pitcher who usually plays in the ninth inning to protect a lead.

contract
A written agreement that keeps a player with a team for a certain amount of time.

debut
First appearance.

minor leagues
A system of leagues for the development of young baseball players.

professional
Paid to do something as a job.

prospects
Players that people expect to do well at a higher level.

rookie
A first-year player.

veteran
A player who has spent several years in a league.

TO LEARN MORE

Books

Adamson, Thomas K. *Juan Soto*. Minneapolis: Bellwether Media, 2023.

Hewson, Anthony K. *Washington Nationals*. Minneapolis: Abdo Publishing, 2023.

Kortemeier, Todd. *San Diego Padres*. Minneapolis: Abdo Publishing, 2023.

More Information

To learn more about Juan Soto, go to **pressboxbooks.com/AllAccess.**

These links are routinely monitored and updated to provide the most current information available.

INDEX

All-Star Game, 24

Boston Red Sox, 23

Chirinos, Robinson, 5-6

Hader, Josh, 17
Home Run Derby, 21
Houston Astros, 5-6

Judge, Aaron, 26

Kershaw, Clayton, 17

Los Angeles Dodgers, 17, 26

Milwaukee Brewers, 15, 17

Rendon, Anthony, 17
Rodríguez, Julio, 21

Seattle Mariners, 21
Soto, Elian, 9, 12

Verlander, Justin, 6

Williams, Ted, 23-24